Mayer
dak, Heather C.,
car F. Mayer : hot dog manufacturer

.07

# Food Dudes

# OSCAR F. MAYER

## Hot Dog Manufacturer

Heather C. Hudak

Checkerboard
Library

An Imprint of Abdo Publishing
www.abdopublishing.com

# abdopublishing.com

Published by Abdo Publishing, a division of ABDO, PO Box 398166, Minneapolis, Minnesota 55439. Copyright © 2018 by Abdo Consulting Group, Inc. International copyrights reserved in all countries. No part of this book may be reproduced in any form without written permission from the publisher. Checkerboard Library™ is a trademark and logo of Abdo Publishing.

Printed in the United States of America, North Mankato, Minnesota
062017
092017

THIS BOOK CONTAINS
RECYCLED MATERIALS

Production: Mighty Media, Inc.
Editor: Rebecca Felix
Cover Photographs: Shutterstock (main); Wisconsin Historical Society, WHS-67547 (inset)
Interior Photographs: AP Images, p. 27; Getty Images, p. 21; iStockphoto, p. 25; Library of Congress, pp. 9, 11; Shutterstock, pp. 4, 5, 18; Wikimedia Commons, p. 7; Wisconsin Historical Society, WHS-116260, p. 19; Wisconsin Historical Society, WHS-19872, p. 13; Wisconsin Historical Society, WHS-67546, p. 15; Wisconsin Historical Society, WHS-67547, p. 1; Wisconsin Historical Society, WHS-84447, p. 17; Wisconsin Historical Society, WHS-99333, p. 23

**Publisher's Cataloging-in-Publication Data**

Names: Hudak, Heather C., 1975-, author.
Title: Oscar F. Mayer: hot dog manufacturer / by Heather C. Hudak.
Other titles: Hot dog manufacturer
Description: Minneapolis, MN : Abdo Publishing, 2018. | Series: Food dudes |
　　　Includes bibliographical references and index.
Identifiers: LCCN 2016962521 | ISBN 9781532110825 (lib. bdg.) |
　　　ISBN 9781680788679 (ebook)
Subjects: LCSH: Mayer, Oscar F., 1859--1955--Juvenile literature. | Oscar Mayer
　　　& Co. (Firm)--United States--Biography--Juvenile literature. |
　　　Businesspeople--United States--Biography--Juvenile literature.
Classification: DDC 641.6 [B]--dc23
LC record available at http://lccn.loc.gov/2016962521

# Contents

# Young Oscar

No ball game or barbecue would be the same without an Oscar Mayer hot dog. But who is to thank for these **fantastic** franks? Oscar Mayer is more than a brand. He was the man behind one of the most successful meat companies in the United States.

Oscar F. Mayer was born in the German state of Bavaria on March 29, 1859. His mother was Wilhelmina Wagner. His father was Ferdinand Mayer. Oscar had two brothers, Gottfried and Max. When Oscar was 11 years old, Ferdinand died. Oscar left school and went to work to help support his family.

Oscar's cousin John Schroll owned a grocery store in the Bavarian city of Munich. Oscar worked there for the next three years. Then, in 1873, Schroll closed the store. He thought there was more opportunity in the United States and decided to move his family there. Fourteen-year-old Oscar asked his mother for **permission** to go with his cousin. Wilhelmina agreed.

With Oscar in tow, the Schroll family settled in Detroit, Michigan. Oscar soon found a job at a butcher shop. In 1876, he accompanied the Schrolls when they moved to Chicago, Illinois. Schroll opened a drugstore there. Oscar took a job working as an **apprentice** at a meatpacking business called Armour & Company.

*Munich, where Oscar's cousin owned a grocery store, is the capital of Bavaria.*

# Getting Started

Armour & Company was an important business in Chicago. It was known for its **unique** butchering methods. Unlike other meatpacking companies, it did not throw away any parts of the animal. This helped shape meatpacking industry practices in the United States at the time.

Mayer learned a lot during his time at Armour & Company. He began developing ideas for starting his own meat business. In 1880, Mayer shared his ideas with his younger brother, Gottfried, who was back in Germany.

Oscar also asked Gottfried to begin studying sausage making. Sausages are a traditional German food. Gottfried studied the sausage-making process. He also learned how to **cure** ham. Meanwhile, Oscar began saving money for his dream.

By 1883, Oscar had saved enough money to start his own business. He rented a failing meat market and sausage-making shop called Kolling Meat Market. It was located in a German neighborhood in Chicago. At the time, about 25 percent of people in Chicago were German. The Mayers **catered** to their tastes.

Armour & Company played a role in helping Chicago become the center of the US meatpacking industry.

Meanwhile, Gottfried and Max had moved to Chicago to live and work with their brother. Mayer named his shop Oscar Mayer and Brothers Company. The brothers' specialties were wieners and sausages. Germans who lived in the neighborhood loved Gottfried's sausages. They reminded them of the traditional foods they ate in Germany. The brothers' small shop quickly became popular with locals. Business was booming.

# Moving Up

As Mayer's shop expanded, so did his family. In 1887, he married Louise Christine Greiner. The two had one son and four daughters. Life was good at home and in business.

The Mayers' shop continued to be busy. The building's landlord took notice. In 1888, he decided to take the shop back over, hoping that customers would continue to visit the location to shop for their meats. So, the Mayer brothers found a new location just two blocks away. Their customers followed them, putting the brothers' former landlord out of business within the year.

The two-story shop where the Mayer brothers worked also served as their home. The shop was located on the first floor. The Mayers lived upstairs.

Max did the company's bookkeeping. Mayer and Gottfried focused on making meats and running the shop. The brothers continued to make German sausages and other traditional meats.

Over the next few years, the Oscar Mayer and Brothers Company continued to grow. It began **sponsoring** events, mainly those for people of German descent, such as **polka** band

In the late 1800s and early 1900s, people bought their food from several sources. This included butchers, grocers, and dry goods stores.

**expositions**. The Mayers set up displays at these events to promote their company. It wasn't long before Oscar Mayer became a well-known name in meats around the city.

# Quality Goods

The Oscar Mayer and Brothers Company continued to grow. It employed 43 people, 8 of whom were salespeople. Each salesperson drove a horse and wagon filled with Oscar Mayer meat products. They delivered to nearly 300 stores across Chicago and parts of Wisconsin.

At the time, it was rare for salespeople to tell customers who supplied the products they purchased. Customers received plainly wrapped packages and never knew where the foods inside came from. But Mayer was proud of the quality he provided. He wanted people to be able to identify the meats he made. So, in 1904, he began labeling his meat packages.

Mayer had another chance to promote his company's quality in 1906. That year, US President Theodore Roosevelt passed the Federal Meat Inspection Act. It required all meatpacking businesses to meet certain standards. Mayer volunteered his company as one of the first to take part in government inspections.

The inspections **confirmed** the quality of Oscar Mayer meats. Officials declared the meats were properly made in clean and

US President Theodore Roosevelt signed the first federal laws to regulate foods in the United States.

healthy conditions. Mayer was proud of this report. He added a government seal of approval to his packaging. This helped boost the success of his meats even more.

# Changes & Success

The Mayer brothers had proven to be excellent business owners. Their company ran smoothly year after year, earning new customers and more profit. In 1917, the company became even more well known when it began placing ads in newspapers. The ads showed that Oscar Mayer was a brand approved by the US government.

By 1919, the company was stable and the brothers were able to shake things up a bit. They changed the company name to Oscar Mayer & Company. They also opened another plant in Madison, Wisconsin.

The company began making changes in its product line too. It added new varieties of sausages, bacon, and ham. It also tested out new ways of packaging foods so they stayed fresh. These packages preserved the meat for longer, making it possible to ship meats for sale across the entire country.

Another big packaging change came in 1924. That year, Oscar Mayer & Company began selling pre-wrapped, sliced bacon. The plastic packaging was transparent, allowing the customers to see the packaged meat. It was the first of its kind on the US market.

The Mayers also began selling brand-name bundles of hot dogs.  Every fourth hot dog was wrapped in a yellow band that had the Oscar Mayer name on it.  The label also had the government seal of approval.

*Oscar Mayer's pre-wrapped, sliced bacon became one of its most popular products.*

# New Generation

Mayer successfully led the Oscar Mayer company for 45 years. In 1928, he handed over the job of president to his son, Oscar G. Mayer. Mayer took on the role of Oscar Mayer & Company chairman of the board.

Oscar G. had worked in his father's store as a child, taking orders and making deliveries. After high school, he went to Harvard University in Massachusetts to study business. Oscar G. graduated in 1909 and joined the family business soon after. Like his father, he worked his way up. He learned many different jobs before taking over as the company's leader.

Under Oscar G.'s leadership, the company was more successful than ever. When he became president, Oscar Mayer & Company had been well known in Chicago and the surrounding area. But Oscar G. made the company a household name across the nation. He began bigger advertising campaigns, developed new products, and made products available across the country.

Oscar G. was president
of the Institute of
American Meat Packers
from 1924 to 1928.

# The Wienermobile

The Oscar Mayer company saw continued success thanks to Oscar G.'s strong leadership. But the company's **marketing** efforts in the 1930s also played a large role in its growth. Some Oscar Mayer advertisements became famous around the world.

In 1936, Oscar Mayer company created Little Oscar. This was a company **spokesperson** in the form of a chef character. A man was hired to dress up like Little Oscar and go to different events to talk about Oscar Mayer products. People loved Little Oscar.

That same year, Oscar G.'s cousin, Carl Mayer, came up with a special kind of car for Little Oscar to drive. The car was 13 feet (4 m) long and looked like a giant hot dog on wheels. It also had the Oscar Mayer logo on its side.

Oscar Mayer company named its special car the Wienermobile. Little Oscar drove the Wienermobile in local parades and around Chicago. People would get excited to spot the vehicle and Little Oscar. They would line up to have their picture taken with them.

Little Oscar and the Wienermobile became famous in Chicago. Soon, the rest of the country was introduced to the Wienermobile through television commercials. A cartoon **version** of Little Oscar appeared in commercials and ads. The increased exposure only made the character and vehicle more popular.

Oscar Mayer company calls its Wienermobile drivers Hotdoggers.

# Breakthroughs

Oscar Mayer's **marketing** efforts weren't the company's only advancement. It also experimented with new types of packaging equipment and performed food research in the 1940s. It developed a **unique** product called Slice Pak in 1950.

Slice Pak was a type of packaging with a vacuum seal. Exposure to air ages food, eventually causing it to spoil. The vacuum seal kept air out of the packages. This kept the meats inside fresh for days longer.

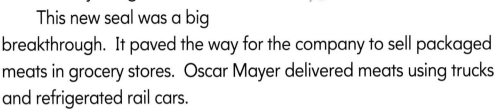

This new seal was a big breakthrough. It paved the way for the company to sell packaged meats in grocery stores. Oscar Mayer delivered meats using trucks and refrigerated rail cars.

Oscar Mayer & Company saw another change when Mayer died on March 11, 1955, at the age of 95. Oscar G. stepped down as president and into his father's former role of chairman of the board. Oscar G.'s son, Oscar G. Mayer Jr., became company president.

*Oscar G. Jr. gives a speech to company employees in Madison in 1964.*

Oscar G. Jr. had graduated from Cornell University in New York in 1934. He went on to study at Harvard Business School for one year. Then, he left school to help with the family business. Oscar G. Jr. learned many jobs at the family company before taking over as president.

With Oscar G. Jr. at the helm, the company opened more than 30 US sales and distribution centers by the 1960s. It became the top brand-name meat manufacturer in the United States. In 1961, Oscar Mayer & Company began operating outside the United States as well. It bought a meat-processing company in Venezuela.

# Happy Tunes

As Oscar Mayer & Company expanded to new physical locations, it was also taking over another medium. By the 1950s, television and radio were popular in many US homes. For years, Oscar Mayer had aired television commercials and radio ads. In the 1960s, it created a radio ad in the form of a jingle. The jingle was wildly popular and became one of the most memorable in history.

The Oscar Mayer jingle made its **debut** in 1963, on a Houston, Texas, radio station. The jingle was called "I Wish I Were an Oscar Mayer Wiener," and it was very catchy. Many people thought the jingle was a new hit song, not an ad for hot dogs!

Listeners liked the Oscar Mayer jingle so much, they would call radio stations and ask them to play it. Soon, radio stations across the country were playing the tune. The jingle ad was played until 2010. It was the longest continuously running ad in US history.

Oscar Mayer debuted another jingle in 1974. It was called "The **Bologna** Song" and it was just as catchy as the first song. The opening **lyrics** were, "My bologna has a first name, it's O-S-C-A-R. My bologna has a second name, it's M-A-Y-E-R."

The Oscar Mayer wiener jingle is still popular today! A student sings the song in a 2002 contest.

# Expanding Markets

The Mayer family had built a meatpacking empire, and a brand that was known worldwide. For more than 80 years, a family member had always been president of the company. That changed in 1965, following the death of Oscar G.

As his father had before him, Oscar G. Jr. stepped down from his role as president. He then took over as chairman of the board. A man named P. Goff Beach became president of Oscar Mayer & Company. Until then, Beach had served as the company's vice president.

Beach did well in his new role. The 1970s were a time of much growth for the company. The **decade** started with Oscar Mayer & Company buying the Claussen Pickle Company. Soon after, it opened a new Oscar Mayer plant in Nashville, Tennessee.

In 1972, the Oscar Mayer company spread to even more parts of the world. It bought part of a meatpacking business in Japan and one in Spain. It was not long before Oscar Mayer meats were being sold in countries around the world. The company had become fully international.

Oscar G. Jr. presents college scholarships to Madison students. He was very involved in the Madison community, home of the company headquarters for many years.

Beach moved into the role of chairman of the board in 1973. Robert M. Bolz became president in his place. The company's sales continued to climb under the new leadership.

# Brands & Products

In 1975, Oscar Mayer & Company sold $1 billion of products. This was a company record in sales. Two years later, Oscar G. Jr. retired. In 1981, Oscar Mayer & Company was sold to large food manufacturer General Foods for more than $460 million. General Foods also owned other popular brands, such as Kool-Aid brand drink mix and Jell-O brand gelatin.

In 1985, General Foods was bought by another company. Philip Morris Inc. was best known for selling tobacco, but the company's sales began to fall in the 1970s. Philip Morris began looking for other ways to make money. The food industry seemed like a safe bet. As part of General Foods, the Oscar Mayer company became owned by Philip Morris.

Three years later, Philip Morris also bought food manufacturer Kraft, Inc. In 1989, Kraft merged with General Foods to become Kraft General Foods, Inc. The company name was simplified to Kraft, Inc. in 1995. Oscar Mayer became one of the new company's main brands. Throughout its ownership changes, the Oscar Mayer brand appeared unchanged to consumers, and remained popular.

Lunchables are a popular product developed by Kraft in 1988. The meal trays contain Oscar Mayer meat.

# Oscar Mayer Today

Oscar Mayer's new **corporate** home, Kraft Inc., became Kraft Heinz in 2015. It is one of the largest food and beverage companies in the world. It carries more than 200 brands. Eight of these brands each make more than $1 billion in sales per year. Oscar Mayer is one of them.

The company's new owners still employ many of the famous **marketing** tools the Mayers put in place. Today, there are six Oscar Mayer Wienermobiles in existence. Their design hasn't changed much from the original. But they are much larger! Each one is 27 feet (8.2 m) long, making them twice as long as the original.

The Wienermobiles tour the nation, making appearances at special events, schools, and youth camps. Kraft Heinz shares the Wienermobiles' adventures on social media sites such as Facebook and Twitter, urging customers to follow the cars' activity. Over the years, the Wienermobiles have created as much buzz for the Oscar Mayer brand as millions of dollars of ads would.

The quality Mayer established is also still a part of the Oscar Mayer brand. More than 130 years after Oscar F. Mayer founded his company, Oscar Mayer meats are still a top choice among people around the world. The company has expanded to sell deli meats, bacon **jerky**, meat snack packages, and more. People know Oscar Mayer is a name they can trust for top-quality foods.

The Wienermobile celebrated its seventy-fifth birthday in 2011. People still get excited when they spot the giant hot dog in their hometowns.

# Timeline

**1859** — Oscar F. Mayer was born in Bavaria, Germany, on March 29.

**1873** — Mayer moved to the United States with his cousin John Schroll.

**1883** — Mayer rented a shop with his brothers and started his own meat business.

**1904** — Mayer began labeling his company's meats so customers could tell them apart from competitors' meats.

**1919** — The company opened a second plant in Madison, Wisconsin.

**1924** — Mayer started selling pre-wrapped, sliced bacon.

**1936** — Little Oscar became the company's spokesperson, and the Wienermobile was introduced.

**1955** — Oscar F. Mayer passed away on March 11, at the age of 95.

**1963** — The Oscar Mayer wiener jingle debuted on a radio station in Houston, Texas.

**1974** — "The Bologna Song" was released.

# Lively Lyrics

Have you heard the famous Oscar Mayer jingles?  Ask an adult to help you search for the commercials online to hear the songs and lyrics.  Below are the first lines of each song.  Can you sing the rest of them?

## "I Wish I Were an Oscar Mayer Wiener"

Oh, I'd love to be an Oscar Mayer wiener

That is what I'd truly love to be . . .

## "The Bologna Song"

My bologna has a first name,

it's O-S-C-A-R.

My bologna has a second name . . .

# Glossary

**apprentice** - a person who learns a trade or a craft from a skilled worker.

**bologna** - a large, smoked sausage made of various finely ground meats, such as beef and pork.

**cater** - to provide food.

**confirm** - to definitively state or prove true something that was previously uncertain.

**corporate** - relating to a large business or organization made up of a group of people who have the legal right to act as one person.

**cure** - to prepare meat so that it can be saved for future use.

**debut** - to officially introduce a first appearance.

**decade** - a ten-year period.

**exposition** - a show or exhibition open to the public.

**fantastic** - very excellent or wonderful.

**jerky** - meat that has been preserved in long, dried slices.

**lyrics** (LIHR-ihks) - the words of a song.

**marketing** - the process of advertising or promoting an item for sale.

**permission** - when someone in charge says it is okay to do something.

**polka** - a fast-paced and lively dance that originated in central Europe.

**spokesperson** - a person who is responsible for speaking for a group or organization.

**sponsor** - to pay for a program or an activity in return for promoting a product or a brand.

**unique** (yoo-NEEK) - being the only one of its kind.

**version** - a different form or type of an original.

# Websites

To learn more about Food Dudes,
visit **abdobooklinks.com**.  These links are routinely monitored
and updated to provide the most current information available.

# Index